Process Theology

Embracing Adventure with God

Bruce G. Epperly

Topical Line Drives, Volume 5

Energion Publications
Gonzalez, FL
2014

ISBN10: 1-63199-002-0
ISBN13: 978-1-63199-002-1

Energion Publications
P. O. Box 841
Gonzalez, FL 32560

energionpubs.com
pubs@energion.com

In Gratitude

to my teachers John Cobb, David Griffin, Bernard Loomer,
Richard Keady, and Marie Fox
and South Congregational Church, Centerville, MA,
a congregation where God is still speaking
and the process continues.

1

What Is Process Theology and Why Is It Important?

Susan came to my study with a spring in her step. For several weeks, this inquisitive and intelligent young mother had met with me for conversations about God. She had come from a conservative Christian background which discouraged her questions and doubts as a sign of unbelief. Her childhood pastor asserted that all the answers she needed were found in a literal understanding of the King James Bible. He regularly pitted the Bible against science, psychology, literature, and the follies of human reason. She was taught at an early age that only faithful Bible-believing Christians were saved. Despite their good works and commitment to their spiritual traditions, everyone else, including more liberal Christians, was doomed to eternal damnation unless they accepted Christ as their personal savior and subscribed to an inerrant understanding of scripture.

Susan could no longer accept what she perceived to be the narrow vision of faith she had learned as a child. She loved Jesus, but had outgrown the faith of her childhood and saw no alternatives to the old time religion of her youth. When she sought my counsel, she wondered if she could still call herself a Christian.

But, now, two months after our first meeting, Susan greeted me with excitement. "I think I get it now. Christianity is different than I thought it was. I *really* am a Christian! I'm just different from my parents and pastor. Following Jesus doesn't mean believing outdated creeds or literal understandings of scripture or turning my back on science. I respect my childhood church. But God is so much bigger. I believe God is alive and as real as my next breath. God wants me to grow and explore new ideas. Now I realize that faith is a journey and not a destination, and God is with me with in all my questions and doubts. God's love includes everyone, including people who ask questions and have doubts!"

All I could say in response was "Hallelujah! Praise God," for Susan had found a faith and a God as big as her questions. Susan had discovered that God was intimate, lively, adventurous, and as near as her next breath and her daughters' heartbeats.

What Susan didn't entirely know when she initially sought me out was that the village pastor was also a process theologian. In the spirit of process theology, our conversations were free-wheeling and open-ended, with many possible destinations and no censorship. I accepted her where she was and invited her to be comfortable exploring new visions of God and herself. While I didn't try to convince her about the superiority of my theological vision, I invited her to imagine God as intimate, relational, and creative. I asked her to ponder the possibility that the future is open not just for us but also for God. I asked her to consider the possibility that God is constantly at work in the world inspiring us to be partners in creating a better world. In contrast to her childhood pastor, I invited her to see the relationship between science and religion as a creative dialogue and explore the possibility that God's revelation comes to people from other cultures and spiritual traditions and not just to Christians.

In the months following her theological epiphany, Susan began reading process theology. She had many questions and struggled with the contrasts between process theology and the faith of her childhood church. But, one afternoon she asserted, "I am so grateful for your introducing me a new way of looking at God and the world. I feel like I'm coming home to a God I can believe in. I don't have to be afraid of my doubts. I see faith as an ongoing adventure with God right beside me, challenging me with new ways of looking at things. God is real to me again. God is right here in your study and down on the beach. I can find God wherever I go, listening and sharing, and growing along with me." Susan had rediscovered a living God through encountering the welcoming spirit of process theology.

The Origins of Process Theology. Theology has always been connected with philosophical reflection. One of the greatest theologians, Augustine of Hippo (354-430 CE), was shaped by Greek philosophical ideas of perfection, meditated through the thought of the philosopher Plotinus and Neoplatonism. He struggled to connect the lively embodiment of Hebraic spirituality and Jesus' ministry with the neo-Platonic definition of perfection as unchanging and embodiment as a hindrance to spiritual growth. Another great Christian theologian Thomas Aquinas (1225-1274) was influenced by Aristotle, who described the ultimate reality as the Unmoved Mover. Any change in God or influence from the changing world on God's experience constituted a diminishment of divine perfection. Aquinas also struggled to join the unchanging divinity of Greek thought with the lively, intimate and emotional God of the Bible, embodied most fully in the Suffering Savior, Jesus of Nazareth. The parents of the Protestant Reformation Martin Luther (1483-1546) and John Calvin (1509-1564) saw God as dynamic and active in the world, but also struggled with the character of divine knowledge and power. Their understandings of divine perfection required God to have active foreknowledge and foreordination in relationship to the events of the world. Nothing new could possibly happen to God nor could the world determine any aspect of God's experience. Their vision of divine activity demanded either: 1) that God predestine in advance all the events of history, including the fate of humans as saved and damned or 2) that God choose those who were saved in an eternal vision, while overlooking the unsaved entirely. As a result of their understandings of divine knowledge, power, and grace, they saw humans as powerless to effect anything positive apart from divine initiative and determination.

Process theology is also philosophically driven, but its philosophical foundations emphasize movement, change, relationship, possibility, creativity, freedom, and open-endedness. Process theologians see the origins of process thought as two-fold. First, they see the Bible as the primary inspiration of process theology. The biblical tradition envisions God as intimate, active in history, and capable of changing course in response to human decisions. God's mercies are new every morning. God's redemptive vision is reflected in God's innovative actions to restore the fortunes of Israel and broaden the scope of salvation to include the whole earth. The prophetic tradition, described by Jewish theologian Abraham Joshua Heschel in terms of the "divine pathos," saw God as intimately involved in the smallest details of economics, politics, and spirituality. Process theologians also see Jesus as a model for process-relational thought. As the word made flesh, Jesus testifies to the goodness of embodiment and the importance of the historical process. Jesus' revelation of God's nature points to a vision of God as intimate, suffering and celebrating, supporting human freedom and creativity, and inviting us to do great things as God's partners in healing the world.

In addition to scripture, process theologians affirm the significance of the British philosopher Alfred North Whitehead (1861-1947) in the formation of process theology. The son of an Anglican clergyman, Whitehead became an agnostic early in his adulthood. He struggled with religious and scientific dogmatism and as a mathematician rejected religious systems that turned their backs on the insights of scientific thinking, whether in the theory of evolution or the emerging relativity theory. Following the death of a whole generation of young Englishmen, including one of his two sons, in World War I, Whitehead began to reconsider his religious agnosticism. While he always recognized the relativity and tentativeness of religious doctrines, Whitehead discovered the need for a vision of God congruent with the evolving understanding of the universe described by physics and biology. For Whitehead, God is the ultimate source of possibility and human creativity. God also insures that no event in the historical process is ever lost. In the divine memory, Whitehead's son and all those who perished in World War I would live forever and, in so doing, influence the ongoing historical process. During his two decades of teaching at Harvard

University, Whitehead set the stage for the emergence of process theology by influencing the philosopher Charles Hartshorne and a generation of theologians, many of whom studied or taught at the University of Chicago - Henry Nelson Weiman, John B. Cobb, Bernard Loomer, and Bernard Meland - and through their impact an ongoing procession of process theologians, including David Griffin, Marjorie Suchocki, Joseph Bracken, Bernard Lee, Norman Pittenger, Clark Williamson, Catherine Keller, Rita Nakashima Brock, Jay McDaniel, and myself. Today, hundreds of pastors and chaplains share the insights of process theology in their pulpits, study groups, and pastoral care. Process theology remains one of the most vibrant forms of theological reflection and has significantly influenced emerging and post-modern Christianity, environmental theology, the interplay of science and religion, feminist and liberation theology, and holistic, earth and body affirming forms of spirituality.

Essential Concepts of Process Theology. One of the parents of process theology, Bernard Loomer, described this novel and innovative way of thinking of God and the world as "process-relational" theology. These two words capture the heart of process thought, whether we are describing the nature of God, the God-world relationship, human life, the non-human world, ethics and spiritual formation, the relationship of science and religion, or survival after death.

I believe that theology is best learned through the interplay of 1) affirmations or positive statements about our deepest beliefs, and 2) spiritual practices that enable us to experience the deepest and most pervasive realities that shape our lives and inspire our personal growth and ethical commitments. Briefly put, process theology can be described through the following affirmations:

1) *The world is a dynamic process.* Life involves constant change and movement. Time is, as the hymn says, "an ever-flowing stream" in which each moment arises, perishes, and gives birth to successors. God is alive and constantly doing things,

bringing forth imaginative possibilities in the human and non-human worlds.

2) *All living things exist in relationship with one another.* We live in an interdependent universe in which each moment of experience arises from its environment, whose influence provides both limits and possibilities. Each moment of our lives also contributes to the larger community and the future beyond itself, whether our personal future or the communities of which we are members.
3) *Experience is universal, though variable, and extends beyond humankind.* While creatures differ in complexity and impact on the world, every creature has some minimal level of responsiveness to its environment. Process theology affirms that consciousness is the tip of the experiential iceberg. Beneath everyday consciousness, our lives are also shaped through unconscious experiences that emerge primarily through dreams and the mutual influence and continuity of mind and body. More than this, non-humans also experience their worlds, some consciously, others primarily unconsciously. This reality of conscious experience among non-humans is obvious in terms of our companion animals in relation to which we enjoy loving and intimate relationships. But, less obvious and just as real are unconscious experiences and relationships at the cellular and molecular levels. The Psalmist proclaims that the heavens declare the glory of God and everything that breathes can praise God. (See especially Psalm 148 and150.) Jesus affirms God's love for sparrows and lilies of the field and the Apostle Paul asserts that God's Spirit groans in the experiences of humans and non-humans alike. Dead and objective matter is an abstraction; concrete actuality is relational and experiential. God, accordingly, can touch every creature from the inside.
4) *The universality of experience leads to the recognition that every creature is inherently valuable and deserves moral consideration.* Process theology values all creation, even apart from its impact on human life. Although, we are often at cross-purposes with

other humans in times of war or in difficult decisions regarding the termination of a pregnancy or the accessibility of medical and governmental services, nevertheless, other humans have value that we must ethically consider. This also applies to our relationships to non-humans. Species, flora and fauna, are valuable not just because we appreciate their beauty but because they experience some level of joy and sorrow. They matter to God and, accordingly, should enter into our own moral calculations. This has led some process theologians to become vegetarians and others, like myself, to purchase meat and poultry that is free range rather than factory farmed.

5) *Freedom and creativity are essential to reality.* We are all artists of our experiences, creating our current experiences from the environment around us, including our own previous experiences and decisions. Even though the past can be the source of limitation, our past experiences do not fully determine our future responses. In fact, the concrete impact of the past is the womb of possibility and creativity. As psychiatrist Viktor Frankl asserted in light of his experiences in a Nazi concentration camp, they can take everything away from a person except her or his ability to choose her or his response to the circumstances of life.
6) *The future is open-ended and we have a role in shaping the future, for good or ill.* The processes of human creativity and history are not determined in advance. Although past decisions made by God and humankind condition and may to greater or lesser extent guide the historical process, there is no predetermined goal to human or planetary history. Along with the Creator, we are creating history as we go along.
7) *God is the primary example of the dynamic, process-relational nature of reality.* God is embedded in the ever-changing and evolving historical process, shaping and being shaped by the universe with which God constantly interacts. Constantly creating in relationship to the world, God is also constantly receiving the influence of historical events. God can be

described as the "most moved mover" or the primary example of what John Cobb and David Griffin describe as "creative-responsive love." God creates but also receives; God is the ultimate agent and also the ultimate recipient of value.

Process theology is lively, historical, relational, and creative. It can transform the way you look at God and the world around you.

2

God in Process

Steve was angry and confused. His ten year old son had just been diagnosed with leukemia. In shock, he sought the guidance of a spiritual counselor, associated with a local new age health clinic. The counselor advised that the family seek the services of an energy worker and use affirmations along with chemotherapy, and then concluded the appointment with a spiritual zinger: "I think that your son's cancer is the result of decisions he made in a past life. At the spirit level, he has lessons he needs to learn and cancer will be his teacher. I don't think he'll get well unless the whole family begins to practice positive healing affirmations."

Although he describes himself as "spiritual but not religious," Steve sought me out because of my reputation in the community as seeker friendly. Steve believed in the power of the mind to shape reality, but this was just too much. "My little boy is so precious. He's innocent of any wrong doing. I can't believe that she's blaming him for his cancer."

A week later, I had a synchronous encounter at a local coffee house. Noticing that I was reading a book on spirituality, Terri, another patron at the coffee house asked me if I attended church and when I noted I was the pastor of the local Congregational church, she began to share her story. "I just left my church," noting a large fundamentalist church in Eastern Massachusetts, "because the pastor told me that my chronic fatigue and depression came from God. He said God was testing my faith, and placing an obstacle in my way, to encourage me to depend on Him alone. He told me that if I had enough faith, I could tell the mountain of depression to go away and it would." The pastor confidently asserted that when she had enough faith, she could throw away the medications she was taking. Following his counsel, Terri attended prayer services and sought inspiration from scripture, but still struggled with ongoing depression and fatigue. When she reported her continuing ailments to her pastor, he chided her once more for her lack of faith and told her that if only she had more faith and immersed herself in scripture, she would get well. "I can't believe that God is using illness to strengthen my faith and if He is, I'm sure failing. I can't accept that God has a measuring stick for faith and won't cure me unless I reach a certain mark."

Reimagining Power. It has been said that theology begins in the midst of pain that causes our usual certainties and sense of divine favor to collapse. We want relief, and we also want to know where God is in the pain we experience. The reality of suffering, whether it involves Syrian refugee children, a child's cancer, or a tsunami that kills thousands but somehow spares us invites heartfelt questions such as: Does God have a purpose for our suffering? Is our suffering the result of God's will or punishment for sin? Is there a spiritual formula that will help me get well? Why was he spared while my daughter died?

The realities of pain and evil challenge God's existence; but more importantly, they also beg the questions: If God exists, what kind of God is at work in our lives? Is God on our side or against us? Is God apathetic and emotionally distant or does God truly feel our pain? Does God fully determine the events of our lives or are there free play, accident, and human agency in the universe? Do our prayers matter and if so, what difference do they make?

Power and relationship are interdependent. Process theologian Bernard Loomer cites two kinds of power, unilateral and relational. For some theologians, everything comes from the hand of God. God has all the power, shaping every event in entirety according to God's eternal, perfect, and unswerving will. Others see God having the power to create a perfect world, but permitting evils to occur to deepen our faith or to serve God's greater purposes. In his best-selling *Purpose Driven Life,* Christian writer Rick Warren states that God has chosen all the important events of our lives, from

DNA and family origin to traumatic experiences and unexpected successes, without our input. God is the potter and we are the clay. God is at work in the cancer that may kill us and the physician's ingenuity that may save us. Everything is driven by God's purposes and both positive and negative events serve as tests of our faith and stewardship. If we pass the test, we experience God's saving love; however, if we fail, then we are alienated from God now and in eternity. From Warren's perspective, God's will is inexorable and is executed in our lives and the world, with or without, our conscious participation. Sovereignty is the primary characteristic of God's relationship with the world.

In contrast, process theology sees relationship as primary in God's interactions with the world. God acts within the world to bring about the best possibilities in every situation. God does not determine everything, but presents a vision of beauty and the energy to achieve it for every moment of experience. God truly loves the world, seeking to maximize freedom, creativity, and value appropriate to our particular context. In the spirit of the Apostle Paul's affirmation, "in all things God works for good" (Romans 8:28), God moves within the circumstances from which our lives emerge, bringing forth possibilities for creative transformation. We must, in concert with our environment, strive to embody these values to fully experience God's vision. Still, even when we fail, God continues to provide opportunities for healing and wholeness.

God creates and also responds. Our actions can either enhance or diminish God's presence in the world, shaping the texture of God's activity in the world. God is constantly adapting to the world as it is, presenting relevant visions of what this world can be. As the reluctant prophet Jonah discovers, God changes God's mind when Nineveh repents. This same phenomenon is at work in Jesus' healing ministry: a woman's deep faith awakens Jesus' healing power, a persistent foreigner motivates Jesus to heal her daughter, and a circle of companions makes the difference between life and death for a twelve year old girl.[1] Conversely, Jesus' ability to heal is limited by the lack of faith of the people of his hometown.

Process thought asserts that God is always at work in the world. But, in contrast to images of divine determinism and predestination, God's power is always relational and contextual, inviting us to become God's partners in healing the world. While many traditional theologies describe the phrase "God's will" in terms of the unilateral unfolding of God's power in the world of earthquakes, auto accidents, and cancer, process theology more accurately captures the meaning of God's will as ethical and spiritual, "thy kingdom come, thy will be done, *on earth as it is in heaven."* Our actions shape the world and our responses to God's vision bring us and the world nearer or farther from the future God envisions for all creation.

An Intimate God. Many Christians speak of having a personal relationship with God. They affirm that "he walks with me and he talks with me and tells me I am his own" even though their theologies describe an objectifying God who has everything planned out in advance or who knows what we will do or say long before we say it. Our prayers mean nothing to such a God: they provide nothing new to God's complete and unchanging awareness of the world.

In contrast, process theology delivers on the promise that God truly hears our prayers, embraces our whole lives, and needs our faithfulness to bring healing the world. Only a dynamic, relational, ever-evolving God can fulfill the Epistle of James' affirmation: "draw near to God and God will draw near to you" (James 4:8).

Every positive relationship has two poles: what is constant and what is constantly changing. A good parent, spouse, partner, or friend is faithful and loving, and this is non-negotiable through all the seasons of life, or as the traditional marriage vows affirm: "for better or for worse, for richer or for poorer, in sickness and in health." The shape of this fidelity is constantly changing. As the grandparent of two small boys, I give them plenty of love and also

1 Bruce Epperly, *Healing Marks: Healing and Spirituality in Mark's Gospel* (Gonzalez, FL: Energion, 2012).

plenty of counsel: "Don't go in the street!" "Stay by my side" "Don't touch the keys on the telephone!" (One of the boys has called 911 more than once!) This is good advice for toddlers; but what would happen if they followed this advice when they went away to college? This same interplay of constancy and change applies to God. In contrast to Aristotle's "unmoved mover," for whom thinking about our changing world or receiving any input from us is a fall from perfection, process theology sees God as the "most moved mover," touched by everything we do, open to all of our feelings, feeling our pain and joy from the inside, and then touching us with love and challenge appropriate to our personal condition. God's faithful changeability is captured in the words of one of my favorite hymns:

> Great is thy faithfulness,
> Great is thy faithfulness
> Morning by morning new mercies I see
> All I have needed thy hand has provided
> Great is thy faithfulness, Lord unto me.

God's faithfulness is grounded in the mutuality of call and response. God calls and we respond, providing God with new possibilities to transform our lives and the world. We call and God responds, dealing with the "real" world of our experience in its complexity, and providing redemptive and healing possibilities for persons and nations. We are free to turn away from God, and bring ugliness and pain to God's experience. But, still God moves in our lives, seeking to lure us home like a shepherd in search of a lost sheep or a parent running to meet a wayward child.

We matter to God. Our experiences change God. God is, as Whitehead asserts, "the fellow sufferer who understands." God is also the faithful companion who rejoices and like the parent of the Prodigal Son, celebrates by providing a feast of new possibilities.

Our prayers matter to God. In an interdependent universe, they shape unconsciously the experiences and environment of those for whom we pray, creating openings for grace and healing energy. They also shape God's experience and open the door for God's tender mercies to bring about positive changes of body, mind, and spirit. Neither our prayers nor God's activity is unilateral and all-determining, but the partnership of God and the world can tip the balance in favor of healing, justice, reconciliation, and redemption. In every moment, God whispers, "Listen! I am standing at the door, knocking; if you hear my voice and open the door, I will come in to you and eat with you, and you with me" (Revelation 3:20). When we answer in the affirmative, we open the door to possibilities that are "more than we can ask or imagine" (Ephesians 3:20).

An Adventurous God. Alfred North Whitehead makes two profound statements that can transform our congregations, communities and lives.

> The worship of God is not a rule of safety — it is an adventure of the spirit, a flight after the unattainable. The death of religion comes with the repression of the high hope of adventure.[2]

> At the heart of the nature of things, there are always the dream of youth and the harvest of tragedy. The Adventure of the Universe starts with the dream and reaps tragic Beauty. This is the secret of the union of Zest with Peace: That the suffering attains its end in a Harmony of Harmonies.[3]

Many people, especially today's young adults, identify religion with the preservation of the status quo. They see the church as the final bastion of opposition to what is most important for our survival: science, awareness of global climate change, and social transformation in quest of justice and equality. The last place they look for adventure is in the church. Yet, the Bible is an adventure story, describing a people's experience of an adventurous God, who

2 Alfred North Whitehead, *Science and the Modern World (New York:Macmillan, 1926), 275.*

3 Alfred North Whitehead, *Adventures of Ideas* (New York: Free Press, 1963), 296.

calls forth the universe, liberates a nation, challenges reluctant spiritual leaders, provokes controversy with new images of faithfulness, overcomes race and ethnicity, and invites followers to get out of their comfort zones and launch out into the depths of life.

Process theology asserts that God is the source of both order and novelty. God is faithful, setting galaxies in motion and working within the natural processes of seedtime and harvest. In response to ecological destruction, God moves to sustain life and inspire environmental awareness and action. God nurtures our cells, souls, and immune system, providing energies of health in the context of trauma and disease. Although the battle is often lost, God still moves, seeking healing among those who grieve the loss of a child, friend, spouse, or partner. God has the patience and resilience to work within the world to embody the centuries-long trajectories characteristic of the moral arc of history.

In preserving the dynamic and evolving order of the universe, God also inspires adventure and calls us to new horizons of scientific discovery, medical research, social justice, and spiritual transformation. Through dreams, visions, hunches, synchronous relationships, burning bushes, and prophetic speech, God inspires us to open to new possibilities for ourselves and the world. Each moment is a potential epiphany. Each moment has a vocation in which we move from the stability of the past to creativity of the present and the future. God cherishes the "old time religion" and so should we. As God challenges us to go beyond "that's the way we've always done it," God also reminds us that the old time religion was once described as new-fangled and criticized for its novelty. God meets us in burning bushes and when we ask for God's name, the Great Mystery responds, "I am what I am becoming." God also comforts us with the promise that "I am with you always" in all the seasons of life (Matthew 28:20).

3

Knowing God

As a child I learned the camp song: "The B-I-B-L-E, Oh, that's the book for me. I stand alone on the word of God. The B-I-B-L-E." I excelled in Bible drills and could find scripture passages faster than anyone in my youth group. I still have the King James Bible that was presented to me when I was baptized in 1961. The Bible is central to my life, but my spiritual journey has challenged my childhood understanding of scripture.

Although he was a Baptist preacher, my Dad was not a biblical literalist. Some of my Sunday School teachers were biblical literalists. They were sure that that the earth was created in six days, less than ten thousand years ago; that women should not be pastors based on a solitary passage in I Corinthians; that Roman Catholics were idolaters because they worshipped the Virgin Mary; and that Jesus would return according to the timetable of biblical prophetic writings. They were also clear that when there was a conflict between scripture and science, the Bible trumped science and human knowledge.

What was not clear to me, as an inquisitive child, involved why we ate ham on Easter even though it was prohibited in scripture and why some of my father's congregants mowed their lawns on Sunday afternoons even though it was the Christian Sabbath. I soon learned that even fundamentalists pick and choose what they follow in scripture. I also discovered that I needed more than the Bible for my own spiritual growth: my faith was strengthened as a result of reading texts from psychologists, novelists, poets, scientists, and sages from other spiritual traditions.

The Meaning of Revelation. Process theology believes that God is still speaking in a variety of ways. In the spirit of John's Gospel, process theology believes that God gives light to all creation and that all humans are personally touched by God's word and wisdom. Revelation is always both personal and global in nature. God's creative word constantly influences us through visions, dreams, possibilities, and synchronous moments.

Process theology also asserts that revelation is always concrete and relational. God reveals wisdom to concrete historical people at particular times and places. Biblical revelation is never abstract; it comes from the voice of a burning bush beckoning to Moses on his way to work; a whispered word to Amos in the vineyard; a multi-sensory revelation to Isaiah in the Temple; a mentor's challenge to Queen Esther; a marvelous encounter of young Mary with an angelic visitor amid her daily tasks; a nocturnal visitor to Joseph in a dream; and a blinding light to Paul on the way to Damascus. While their encounters with God contained global truths, they were also experienced personally and shaped by the historical and personal setting of their receivers. God's revealing word also comes to you and me. God is still speaking and most often experienced in the everyday events of our lives.

Process theology affirms the universality and intimacy of revelation. The heavens declare the glory of God. As the reality in which we live and move and have our being, God shapes all creation: all persons are chosen to receive divine inspiration, appropriate to their life-situation and personal choices. The invisible nature of God is revealed to all creation through the things God has made (Romans 8:20). Although process theology affirms a universal experience of God, process theology equally asserts God's ability to shape revelation to particular people with greater or lesser intensity and focus. While these revelations are not different in kind from the moment by moment experiences we have of God, they are different in their level of revealing God's vision and nature. Like us, God can choose to be more present and dynamic in some settings than others. Still, despite its level of intensity, God's revelation never short circuits the receiver. It comes in ways that build on her or his experiences and reflect her of his highest values.

A Living Bible. Process theology affirms the lively inspiration of scripture. God was at work in the communities that shaped our written scriptures and in the various writers who penned the library of texts we call the Bible. Profoundly historical, biblical inspiration varies from verse to verse and chapter to chapter. Some biblical messages have universal applicability; others are time bound and, frankly, no longer relevant to our current scientific, ethical, and theological understandings.

As a preacher, I recognize that every scriptural passage requires interpretation. Some passages – such as those which encourage violence or describe illness as resulting from God's will or punishment – can be detrimental to persons suffering from serious illness or parents whose children's lives are cut short by cancer or car accidents. Like all media of divine revelation, scripture is variable in insight and helpfulness, mostly due to the vantage point or interests of the receiver. Still, God still speaks in the reading and listening to scripture. Revelation is unfinished and evolving. In the words of Puritan pastor, John Robinson, "God has yet to have more light and more truth to break forth from his holy word." A living bible is always open-ended, subject to interpretation, and inspirational in new and creative ways. As the author of Lamentations affirms: "The steadfast love of God never ceases, God's mercies never come to an end; they are new every morning; great is your faithfulness" (Lamentations 3:22-23).

The Many Voices of God. Process theology affirms the wisdom of John's Gospel, "The true light, which enlightens everyone, was coming into the world." (John 1:9) Everyone receives a portion of divine wisdom and enlightenment. Revelation is not restricted to a particular continent, ethnic group, era, or spiritual tradition. Accordingly, wherever spiritual wisdom is found, God is its source.

The reality of other faith traditions is not a fall from grace, but a reflection of God's love for humankind. Revelation is given to each people and culture according to its particular history, environment, and needs. God moved in the patriarchs, matriarchs, and prophets of the Hebraic people and is still at work in the evolution of Judaism in all its theological and spiritual richness. God revealed God's vision for humankind in the life of Jesus and has inspired, with greater and lesser receptivity, over two thousand years of Christian history. But, God has also whispered in the flowing Ganges and the mountains of Tibet, inspiring sages and gurus. God's vision inspired Gautama to become a world savior and Lao Tzu to share wisdom with the Chinese empire. Mohammed heard God's voice echoing through a cave and Confucius (Master Kung) felt divine inspiration as he sought to nurture a great culture.

The varieties of spiritual experience point to the constancy and intimacy of God's love. Different revelations and understandings of the holy inspire us to go beyond relativism in the quest for greater truth and wisdom. Faith traditions can learn from one another. Despite their histories and cultures, each faith tradition points to certain aspects of the Holy that other traditions can embrace as part of their own evolving history. Christians can learn silent meditation from Buddhists and, in return, share the Hebraic-Christian commitment to prophetic spirituality and social justice. Hindus can share the wisdom of yoga and Christians can witness to the all-embracing healing energy present in Jesus of Nazareth. The journey with God is never-ending and always enriching. There is always more light to be shed on the human adventure because God is alive and constantly revealing new possibilities to us.

4

Christ in a Pluralistic Age

In the late 1976, Campus Crusade launched a bumper sticker campaign, highlighting the words "I Found It" accompanied by the listing of a toll free number for more information. Intended to bring America to Christ, it inadvertently spawned a number of counter bumper stickers: in Hebrew-type lettering, one bumper sticker announced, "We Never Lost It"; another noted, "I Found It and Stepped On It"; and in true California fashion, a third bumper sticker proclaimed, "I Found It and I Smoked It." Perhaps the most perceptive response was "What Is It?" echoing Jesus' questions to his disciples, "Who do people say that I am?" and "Who do you say that I am?"

I always take a moment of intellectual pause whenever I lead a funeral or memorial service that includes the words, "I am the way and the truth and the life." Although I typically omit the following sentence, "No one comes to the Father except through me," it still is on my mind as I ponder how these words of consolation might be heard by mourners, seekers, or non-Christians. Very few passages have been more theologically and spiritually problematic and exclusionary than these words from John 14:6. Taken literally they imply that there is only one way to salvation and the road to salvation only comes through a personal relationship with Jesus. Moreover, the nature of that personal relationship is often described in terms of assent to particular creeds and understandings of Christianity: the inerrancy of scripture, the virgin birth and substitutionary atonement (Jesus died for our sins on Calvary), the bodily resurrection of Jesus, supernatural miracles, and the Second Coming of Jesus. Any deviation from a literal understanding of these principles jeopardizes your position in the lamb's book of life. From this perspective, the circle of salvation pertains to Christians alone: as moral as they may be, Buddhists, Hindus, Muslims, practitioners of Native American religion, and other spiritual seekers are excluded from God's plan of salvation and are destined to an eternity of hell-fire and brimstone.

A Christ for the Cosmos. Process theology takes an entirely different route. Following the prologue to John's Gospel (John 1:1-18), process theology sees Christ as the word and wisdom of God and the source of creative transformation and healing in all things. Christ is not limited to a particular creedal, sacramental, and religious system but is the life-giving reality moving in all things. Christ embraces and inspires every pathway of truth and healing within and beyond the Christian tradition. As John's gospel proclaims, "All things came into being through him, and without him not one thing came into being. What has come into being in him was life, and the life was the light of all people" (John 1:3-4). All people are touched by the presence and power of the reality that is most fully manifest in Jesus of Nazareth. All are included in God's plan of salvation and healing. Again, John affirms, "The true light, which enlightens everyone, was coming into the world" (John 1:9).

Process theology, in its Christian forms, affirms the universality of Christ along with unique gifts of the world's great spiritual traditions and the pathways of seekers in all their variety. God's revelation in Christ takes many forms according to its cultural and historical context. While the spiritual realities described by Buddhists, Jews, Muslims, and Hindus may differ from those described by Christians, ultimately the same energy of love shines through each of them. Process theology affirms all healing paths and responds to them as unique and varied manifestations of the divine. Accordingly, we can grow in spiritual wisdom and stature in dialogue with other religious traditions. God is always more than we can imagine and other traditions can shine the light on aspects of God, absent in our own faith tradition. Process theology's commitment to God's global aim at wholeness avoids both religious imperialism and relativism. God has many faces and we can encounter and respond to other revelations guided and inspired by our experience of God's revelation in Jesus Christ, the healer from Nazareth.

From this perspective, the statement "I am the way and the truth and the life. No one comes to the Father except through me" describes God's initiative in providing ways of salvation appropriate to our particular cultural setting and spiritual needs. God has a unique and personal relationship with each and every person and provides pathways of wholeness through which we can experience our vocation and the fullness of God's presence in our lives.

Jesus of Nazareth as God's Beloved Child. The parent of modern process theology Alfred North Whitehead believed that Christianity needed to reclaim its Galilean origins to address the needs of the modern world. Too often in its history the church confused Christ and Caesar. Jesus became a tool of violence and oppression: the cross became a symbol of conquest, exclusion, and judgment, rather than companionship and healing. As we consider the uniqueness of Jesus, we need to consider 1) Jesus' special relationship with God and 2) the nature of Jesus' ministry.

Process theology affirms the spiritual continuity of Jesus and us. The One who present as the source of order and transformation in all things is also present uniquely and in a superlative way in the life and ministry of Jesus. An early church theologian Irenaeus asserted that "the glory of God is a fully alive person." Jesus was fully alive: in Jesus of Nazareth we see the fullest of God and the fullest expression of humankind within the concreteness of time and space. Jesus' divinity and humanity are one, not in some alien and supernatural manner, but in a naturalistic and relational manner. Irenaeus and his second century theological colleague Clement of Alexandria affirmed, Christ became human so that we might share in divinity.

In describing the experience of the twelve year old Jesus in the Jerusalem Temple, Luke proclaims that Jesus grew "in wisdom and stature and favor with God and humankind." Jesus grew! His humanity was real: he lived in a particular time and place, was ethnically and religiously Jewish, male, and shaped by the realities of Roman oppression. Jesus was never complete in experience or awareness. Jesus learned new things and was touched by human pain. In the maelstrom of human joy and sorrow, and his emotional, spiritual, and intellectual life, Jesus maintained a sense of unity with God. As the gospel of John proclaims, "I and the Father are one" (John 10:30). Process theology sees this unity as a dynamic call and response. God constantly called Jesus, moving energetically in his spiritual life and actions, and Jesus fully responded to God's call in his complete openness to God regardless of the circumstances of life. On the Cross, Jesus asks God to forgive his tormenters. He is one in the spirit of God, fully transparent to God's vision and fully open to God's healing and welcoming love.

Jesus' uniqueness is God's choice as well as Jesus', for God's presence is variable in creation and, like us, God can reveal more of God's nature and purposes in certain situations rather than others. This is not arbitrary or unfair. It is affirmation of the divine personality and vision for humanity and the world. Like God, we may love many people but each relationship has its own uniqueness. My love for my wife Kate, my son, and grandson's transcends every other love. In like manner, God's love for the world found its fullest expression in the carpenter from Nazareth. The word became fully flesh in Jesus as a way of giving life and light to all flesh. Still, process theology asserts, Jesus was not passive in the process. God's call inspired Jesus' freely given response: Jesus said "yes" day by day and moment by moment to God's call and in Jesus' great "yes" he provided a pathway for our healing and wholeness.

For process theologians, the doctrine of atonement reflects God's nearness to humankind and the world. We are saved by God's energy of love, by the life and teachings of Jesus, the pathway he sets before us, and the model of full humanity he presents to us. Jesus creates a field of force that brings healing to persons and institutions. Jesus' death brings healing, not as a result of divine predetermination or the necessity of his death, but as a reflection of God's suffering along with us.

Process theology asserts that Jesus' death was not foreordained, but is the result of his commitment to share God's love with the world. Jesus' death is a matter of his choice to be faithful to God's mission regardless of the consequences. Like Mary his mother and ourselves, he had freedom to say "no" but his great "yes" frees and heals us and shows us the heart of God.

The Pathway of Jesus. While we come to know Jesus by our beliefs about him, we also discover our identity as God's children by following the pathway of the healer and teacher from Nazareth. Process theology affirms the wisdom present in first Christians' description of themselves as the People of the Way. The Way of Jesus is lively, emerging, evolving, and unfinished. As a process theologian, my own path as a follower of Jesus is inspired by Jesus' own vision statements:

> *The Spirit of God is upon me because God has anointed me to bring good news to the poor. He has sent me to proclaim release to the captives and recovery of sight to the blind, to let the oppressed go free, to proclaim the year of God's favor* (Luke 4:18-19).

> *I came that they might have life, and have it abundantly* (John 10:10).

The path of Jesus is filled with adventure and possibility. Anyone who follows Jesus had better prepare for a world of surprises and wonders, not to mention challenge and occasional conflict with the world's values. Jesus promised that his followers would be able to do "greater things" than they could possibly imagine (John 14:12). Jesus did not hoard his power, but gave it away freely, inviting us to live abundantly and claim our role as God's companions in healing the world. Jesus transforms and gives meaning and redemption to our lives by showing us his path of healing, hospitality, and transformation. He invites us to live out his vision in our own time and place. Jesus' vision of love-in-action included healing the sick, welcoming the outcast, raising dead spirits, challenging dead rituals and unjust systems, embracing the vulnerable, and inviting broken spirits to dream again.[4]

However we understand Jesus' cross, it means at the very least God's embrace of our suffering and transformation of our sin into wholeness. Mysterious in nature, the resurrection means that the irrepressible energy of love and the power of God's imagination, moving through ours, can breathe new life into dying spirits and institutions. Christ is alive and invites us to become fully alive, open to possibility and transformed by vulnerability. Christ is everywhere, breathing life into every healthy spiritual path and inviting us to take our role in birthing God's realm "on earth as it is in heaven."

4 For more on Jesus' healing ministry, see *Healing Marks: Healing and Spirituality in Mark's Gospel* (Gonzales, FL: Energion, 2012).

5

Adventures in the Spirit

Today, many people practice multiple spiritualities. They may be active in their congregation or synagogue, but they also practice meditative and healing techniques from other religious traditions and cultures. Sandy is one such a practitioner of what sociologists of religion describe as hybrid or multiple spiritualities. She reads her Bible every morning, but also spends twenty minutes in Christian Centering Prayer along with half an hour of Hindu yoga. She recently learned reiki healing touch, a form of energy work initiated by Japanese spiritual guide Masao Usui. While others might challenge her eclectic spirituality as watering down her Christian faith, Sandy boldly asserts, "I'm a healthier and more focused follower of Jesus as a result of practicing yoga and reiki. I have a greater appreciation for Jesus' healing ministry as a result of Asian spiritual practices."

I can personally identify with Sandy's affirmation of the value of multiple spiritual practices. Learning Transcendental Meditation as a first year college student in 1970 inspired me to return to the Christian church and explore the riches of the Christian spiritual tradition. Each day, I begin the day with Centering Prayer and biblical affirmations. I also regularly practice reiki healing touch to balance and deepen my physical and spiritual energy.[5] I still find Transcendental Meditation helpful and teach both Christian and Buddhist forms of breath prayer in spiritual formation classes at my congregation. My commitment to Christian healing and affirmation of Jesus' healing ministry is inspired and enhanced by

5 Bruce Epperly and Katherine Epperly, *Reiki Healing Touch and the Way of Jesus* (Kelowna: British Columbia, 2005).

my involvement in reiki healing touch and various global forms of complementary medicine. I am a living example of process theology's vision of revelation: wherever truth and healing are present, God is its source. God inspires every healthy spiritual pathway.

Process spirituality is dynamic, embodied, and incarnational. In the spirit of John's Prologue, a text embraced by process theologians as a witness to God's universal revelation, the word and wisdom of God (the Logos) is described as becoming flesh, as taking on a body, and dwelling among us. With the gospel of John, the Genesis creation story, Jesus' healing ministry, and the prophetic tradition of Bible, process theology affirms that the earth, physical existence, and family life are good. We discover God's presence in embracing, rather than fleeing, the realities of embodiment.

Process spirituality is dynamic. God is constantly doing a "new thing" and bringing forth new possibilities and energies in the human life and the surrounding universe. Faithful spirituality seeks to experience God in the everyday acts of parenting, professional life, and politics. Process theology affirms the statement:

> God in all things.
> All things in God.

Jacob's dream of ladder of angels uniquely describes the spiritual orientation of process theology. One evening, Jacob camped out in wilderness with only a stone for a pillow. During the night, he had remarkable dream of a ladder of angels in which angels ascended from earth to heaven and back down to earth again. He awakened with the promise that his descendants would become a great nation. Filled with awe, he called the place Beth-El, the house of God, and exclaimed, "Surely God was in this place and I did not know it" (see Genesis 28:10-19).

Jacob's dream reveals an essential aspect of process theology. Not only is God in this place, right where we are, but God's revelations are earthly as well as heavenly. Notice that the angels are ascending from earth to heaven. Divine omnipresence reminds us that God's realm is in the here and now. God is fully present in our earthly, embodied moments. We don't need to go to heaven to experience everlasting life. Although it is often hidden by our self-interest and busyness, the fullness of God is found in this very moment, caring for an aging parent, putting diapers on a baby, preparing for work, and embracing your loved one. Divine fullness is not backward looking but is always moving forward toward God's horizon of possibility. As the Apostle Paul proclaimed, "Do not be conformed to this world, but be transformed by the renewing of your minds, so that you may discern what is the will of God—what is good and acceptable and perfect" (Romans 12:2). The word takes flesh in our prayers and daily quiet time. The word and wisdom of God are alive, springing forth from our cells as well as our souls, calling us to be part of God's new creation, as we embrace the vision of a lively God, whose "mercies are new every morning."

Spiritual Practices. One of my teachers, Ernie Campbell, professor at Union Seminary in New York and pastor of Riverside Church, profoundly shaped my theological and spiritual life with just one sentence: "There are only two kinds of people in the world: Those who are in God's hands and know it and those who are in God's hands and don't." Process theology proclaims that we are always in God's care and that God is always present and moving in our lives. Every place is Beth-El, the house of God. Accordingly, although God's grace abounds and God is constantly moving in our lives, spiritual practices such as prayer, meditation, healing touch, icons, and physical postures are intended to awaken us to Jacob's affirmation, "God is in this place and I know it." Life is a dynamic call and response in which God calls and we respond. A statement from the United Church of Christ proclaims "God is Still Speaking." Spiritual practices help us experience – learn, love, and live – God's word and wisdom for us today.

Process theology affirms a variety of spiritual pathways to God. Silent breath prayer, simply listening mindfully for God's inspiration, connects us with the still small voice of God. On Easter night, Jesus breathed on his disciples and said, "Receive the Holy Spirit" (John 20:22). Jesus is still breathing in and though us, inspiring and enlivening our spirits to mission in our world. Focusing on a prayer word by practicing Centering Prayer or even Transcendental Meditation also serves a search light to deeper levels of insight and inspiration and enables us to discern God's "sighs too deep for words" moving through our spirits and the world around us. Energetic healing touch joins us God's healing energy and the healing ministry of Jesus, awakening to the dynamic life in which live, move, and have our being.

Our prayer lives can be deepened by sheer silence and attentiveness to the still, small voice of God; we can also experience God in lively worship, clapping our hands, singing joyfully, and opening to a deeper voice of the Spirit speaking through our own voices. God provides many pathways to enable us to encounter the Holy in our time and place.

Contemplation and Action. A plaque on a bench at the Kirkridge Retreat Center in Pennsylvania proclaims "picket and pray." Many Christians struggle with joining prayer and social and ethical concern. They see prayer and meditation as private and individualistic, as pointing toward an ethereal, disembodied, and historically-irrelevant spirituality and action as lively, embodied, and sometimes confrontational. In contrast, process theology affirms a holistic spirituality that joins silence and action, prayer and picketing, contemplation and political involvement. The God we encounter in silence is also, as the Apostle Paul proclaims, the One whose Spirit is groaning in creation. When we turn away from the vulnerable in our midst, we may experience, as Amos threatens, a famine in hearing God's word.

Contemplation gives us perspective and joins us with all creation, including those with whom we contend. Without prayer and contemplation, political and social involvement often becomes polarizing. We are tempted to demonize our opponent and fail to see our own shortcomings. Moreover without moments of stillness and prayer that connect us with the Fount of Every Blessing we become impatient, lose heart, and often suffer compassion fatigue and burnout.

Our prayers are not just solitary. Our meditation and quiet time radiate across the universe creating a positive field of force that contributes to the healing of persons and institutions. In stillness, we receive insights that join us with the vulnerable and suffering in our midst. As we pray with our eyes open and senses awakened, we discover Christ in the least of these. Action deepens prayer, and prayer guides action. In the world described by process theology, our world is transformed prayerfully and our actions enable us to understand God's vision in new ways. When we follow the prophets and Jesus, we will become God's partners, making every place a sanctuary of love and bringing beauty to our good Earth.

6

Process Ethics: On Earth as It Is in Heaven

In the early 1980's, an evangelical student in one of classes at Central Michigan University shared the following encounter with a local farmer from the congregation he attended who had employed him to paint his house. After finishing painting the house, he asked the farmer if he should finish the job by caulking the windows. The farmer replied, "Don't bother. Jesus is coming soon and I won't need to worry about cold winters anymore." I've always wondered how that farmer felt when winter arrived and the cold Michigan winds blew through his home.

When it comes to ethics, some people are so heavenly minded that they are no earthly good. Others are so sure that they know what is right and wrong that they try mandate their moral perspectives on the larger community, whether it be Islamic law or conservative Christian understandings of abortion and birth control. Many persons have left congregations and the Christian faith entirely because of inflexible and often coercive moral positions that hate the sin, but also end up hating the sinner as well. Process ethics asks: Is it possible to have a dynamic-relational ethic that preserves the wisdom of the past and also updates ancient wisdom in light of new insights from theology, science, cosmology, culture, and scripture? Can we have an ethics of "reverence for life," as claimed by Albert Schweitzer, while recognizing the rights of contrasting positions and the reality that life involves destruction as well as nurture? Can we seek God's Shalom on earth as it is in heaven?

Theology and Ethics. Process theology is profoundly practical and concrete. Our visions of reality find their fulfillment and are tested in the complexities of everyday life, personal decision-making, business practices, and governmental priorities. Faith shapes every aspect of our lives: we cannot separate our faith from our family or national budget. As Alfred North Whitehead asserted, "religion on its doctrinal side can thus be defined as a system of general truths that have the effect of transforming character when they are sincerely held and vividly apprehended."[6] Process theology sees ethical decision-making as arising from several key theological and philosophical insights: the interdependence of life, the universality of experience and value, the relational and contextual nature of life, the importance of possibility, and the nature of God as creative and responsive.

The apostle Paul once described the community of faith as the body of Christ in which each part had vocation for the whole, the wellbeing of the whole depended on the proper functioning of all its members, and body as a whole rejoiced in the success and grieved at the suffering of each part. This vision captures the essence of process ethics on the both the personal and corporate levels. A healthy family and a healthy society join order and creativity to nurture the achievement of each individual part and to protect the well-being of the most vulnerable members. There are no self-made individuals. Our success depends on the support of a healthy environment, ecologically, relationally, and institutionally. The task of ethics is to nurture wholeness and beauty of experience at every level. Accordingly, interdependence and individuality can never be separated. Our actions shape the environment and the environment shapes our overall well-being. Morality aims, Whitehead believes, at "greatness of experience" and this can only be achieved in communities of interdependence, affirmation, and creativity.

Interdependent communities involve a constant and dynamic interplay of contrasting and congruent values. Relationship always involves variety, uniqueness, and self-affirmation and this can lead to a conflict of values that is not easily decided. Process theology

6 Alfred North Whitehead, *Religion in the Making* (New York:Macmillan, 1927), 15,

affirms the universality of experience and this makes ethical decisions challenging at times. On the one hand, we need to respect or have reverence for every creature, from spotted owls, cattle, and dolphins to fetuses (unborn children) and comatose adults. Yet, we also recognize that we are constantly making decisions based on our understanding of what is most important to us in any given situation along with the concrete limitations of our particular historical and economic context. For example, process theology does not tell us how to solve the dilemma of abortion, but it does remind us that personal and public decisions must take into consideration the value of both the growing fetus and the experiencing mother. While the experiences of fetuses are less complex than their mothers, fetuses are still able to experience both comfort and pain, and have significant potential value in terms of future possibility. The expectant mother also has moral claims based on her social situation and life plans. Both mother and fetus, along with the interested father, need to be taken into consideration in personal and political decision-making. Decisions relating to abortion are serious and need to be calculated based on the quality of the fetus' future life and its impact on its parents and the society. However, as we seek to minimize the number of abortions, a priority of process ethics, we must equally create an interdependent society that provides economic and health care for mothers and its most vulnerable members.

While rights are ultimately relational and contextual, and not absolute in nature, our ethical priority must, first, be to affirm life and then seek abundant life for every member of society. Here process theology follows the prophetic mandate to care for the least of these, whether the "least" be an unemployed unwed mother, a child without health insurance or healthy diet, an adult with physical handicaps, or a growing fetus.

Have you seen the bumper sticker that announces, "Save the baby humans" in response to the "Save the whales" bumper sticker? Process theology sees an element of truth in both proclamations. On the one hand, process theology affirms the universality of experience – everything that breathes praises God and God's cares for the sparrows, and so should we. Non-humans have value apart from human interests or benefits. We need to make a commitment to preserving non-human species and also to treating farm animals in ways that do not cause unnecessary suffering. "Life is robbery," Whitehead notes. In other words, transformation as well as survival involves destruction, whether through letting go of the past, challenging immoral practices, or eating meat, fish, poultry, fish, and vegetables. Whitehead asserts, however, that our destruction of other life forms needs to be morally justifiable: meat eating needs to be balanced by humane treatment of animals; abortion needs to be balanced by respect for the fetus and her or his level of experience; national defense needs to take into consideration social welfare programs and the inevitable suffering, often among innocents and non-combatants, during time of war.

An ethic of experience respects non-human life, preserves species, and balances human need with care for the environment and non-human life. In an interdependent universe, the well-being of humankind depends on the health of the non-human world, the ambient atmosphere, and flora and fauna. We must consider the least of these, whether they are homeless children, persons with life-threatening illnesses, plankton, or animals placed at risk by human behaviors. Creation is groaning in part as a result of human behaviors, as the Apostle Paul affirms, and deserves our ethical consideration (Romans 8:22).

God-centered Ethics. Process theology sees God and the world as profoundly interdependent. God is the source of possibility and novelty as well as life-supporting tradition and order. God is also the primary recipient of value. As the prayer book affirms, God is the One to whom all hearts are open and all desires known. God is the most moved mover, touching all things and also being touched by all things. God experiences first-hand what we do to the least of these: God feels our joy and our pain, and is the fellow sufferer who understands. God's vision of possibility and impact on the world is shaped by our openness to God's vision of Shalom. Accordingly, we love God by loving creation; creation-ethics and God-centered ethics are one and the same. Mother Teresa of Calcutta is noted for her affirmation: "Do something beautiful for God." Ethics revolves around the question: "Will you do something beautiful for God? Do your actions and the actions of our government add to the beauty or ugliness of the world? Do we bring greater joy or sorrow to God's life?" Ethics involves our impact on one another and the least of these. It also involves our impact on God.

What we do, whether individually or corporately, truly matters to God. It can enhance or limit God's impact on the world. It can support God's vision of beauty "on earth as it is in heaven" or it can stand in the way of God's purposes for our world. The future is not determined, as the Michigan farmer with which I began this chapter believed. It is wide open. The survival of our planet is in our hands, even though God is at work in every moment of experience. Our vocation is to be God's companions in what Jewish mystics called *tikkun 'olam,* "mending the world." We truly can do something beautiful God, whether in Washington DC, our church, or family.

7

Adventures in Immortality

The night my mother died in 1990, my ten year old son had a surprising dream. He dreamed of walking on the Santa Cruz, California beach with my mother. In the course of the walk, my mother told him to say the following words to my father: "Tell Everett everything's ok." My son was asleep and had no knowledge that my mother was in danger of dying during the night. Another friend of mine confessed recently that he had a mystical "near death experience." While experiencing a major heart attack, he experienced his world as filled with light and he felt the nearness of God, received spiritual guidance from Jesus, and encountered his deceased parents and brother.

Popular culture is discovering the afterlife. A growing number of best-sellers describe encounters with God and experiences of heaven. People are no longer afraid of being labeled as religious fanatics or eccentric if they admit to having near death experiences or share their beliefs about heaven or reincarnation. Aging baby boomers are discovering the inevitability of death and are seeking consolation in the possibility of post-mortem adventures. Despite our medical advances, the mortality rate remains 100%. Everyone Jesus cured eventually died.

The universal reality of loss inspired Martin Luther to state that "in the midst of life, we are surrounded by death." But, in light of God's grace, present in the resurrection of Jesus, Luther also asserted, "in the midst of death, we are surrounded by life."

Until recently, process theologians have been relatively silent about life after death. They have been content with affirming "objective immortality," that is, our survival in God's memory. Every moment perishes and every life ends, but everything shapes God's evolving experience and becomes part of God's everlasting relationship with the universe. In God's memory, what perishes in the world will live evermore. Objective immortality matters. God does not forget, but treasures our lives. Still, is this enough? Can we affirm personal and subjective survival after death in ways that inspire commitment to our present lives and the wellbeing of our planet? Can we live boldly today, investing ourselves in this world, guided by trust in everlasting life in companionship with God? I believe that process theology says "yes" to both objective and subjective immortality.

In the paragraphs that follow, I will be sharing my personal vision of everlasting life. I have been one of the most vocal process theologians in the affirmation that our lives are part of an ongoing divine adventure beyond the grave. God is present at the moment of our conception, guides us through the adventures of this lifetime, urging us to rejoice in embodiment and bring healing to our world, and upon our final earthly breath receives us with open arms with visions of future adventures in communion with God and our fellow creatures.

Process theology proclaims that God is the God of the living and the dead. In fact, God is alive and working at the moment of our deaths. Death does not constitute a defeat for God, but is an invitation to a new relationship with God. Process theology affirms that the God who has been urging us forward in this lifetime will continue to do so beyond the moment of death.

Many people contrast this world and the next in terms of value and importance. They see this lifetime as the "front porch to eternity" or devalue this life in comparison to immortality. In contrast, process theology sees God's omnipresence as the source of value in this life and the next. If God is present everywhere and in all things, then this life matters. Moreover, if our identity persists beyond the grave, that is, if our personality, relationships, and history persist, then we are creating the shape of our afterlife as well as the afterlives of others in this lifetime. God is fully present here and God is fully present beyond the grave. Accordingly, our quests for justice, environmental healing, peace among the nations, and the wellbeing of our children and grandchildren matter right now and forevermore as: 1) contributing to the quality of this worldly experience, 2) bringing beauty to God's experience, 3) making a difference to God's everlasting memory, and 4) shaping the quality of their afterlives. Healthy religion joins rather than separates this life and the next. It inspires us to be faithful to God, bringing forth God's realm "on earth as it is in heaven."

Process theology is adventurous and so must our visions of the afterlife. Everlasting life means everlasting growth in which we come to terms with our earthly history, reconcile with our earthly companions, and continue to grow in relationship with God and others. God is not finished with us when we die. God's love to this goes beyond lifetime to embrace our imperfection and even our unbelief, nurturing growth for the next steps of our journey.

Many Christians implicitly believe that death is stronger than God. At death, they believe that our fate is irrevocably sealed and we will enter either heaven or hell. Such theologies admit that God quits loving many of us at death, can do nothing to save us beyond the grave, and is motivated more by retribution than love in evaluating our lives. Process theology takes another path. Everyone is invited into God's everlasting realm. We enter as fully ourselves, near or distant from God's vision of us, and continue to experience God's great "yes" to us in the afterlife. Over time, we will grow in awareness of God, going from glory to glory, and discovering our calling in a realm where grace not alienation is the ultimate reality.

Despite the popularity and proliferation of texts on near death experiences, no can fully describe the afterlife. Process theology sees continuity - experientially, spiritually, communally, and ethically - between this life and the next. While we may not share the same post-mortem dinner tables with our spouses, friends, and relatives, we will be part of an evolving communion of saints, fully alive in the "resurrection of the person" and now living fully within the body of Christ where each of us has a role in the ultimate transformation of heaven and earth. God is alive and God's Spirit lures us toward horizons beyond our wildest dreams. This is the holy adventure of process theology.

Further Reading

Coleman, Monica. *Making A Way Out of Now Way*. Philadelphia: Fortress, 2008.

Epperly, Bruce. *Emerging Process: Adventurous Theology for a Missional Church*. Cleveland, TN: Parson's Porch Books, 2012.

________. *Holy Adventure: 41 Days of Audacious Living (second edition)*. Parson's Porch Books, 2013.

________. *Process Theology: A Guide for the Perplexed*. New York: Bloomsbury T&T Clark, 2011.

Farmer, Patricia Adams. *The Metaphor Maker*. North Charleston, SC: Create Space, 2009.

McDaniel, Jay. *Gandhi's Hope: Learning from Other Religions as a Source of Peace*. Maryknoll NY: Orbis, 2005.

Suchocki, Marjorie. *In God's Presence: Theological Reflections on Prayer*. Duluth, GA: Chalice, 1996.

CPSIA information can be obtained
at www.ICGtesting.com
Printed in the USA
BVHW032213160119
538051BV00001B/21/P

9 781631 990021